MASTERPIECES
OF
QUEEN ANNE
&
GEORGIAN
FURNITURE

EARLY GEORGIAN CARVED AND GILDED WALNUT ARCHITECTURAL HIGHBOY. Victoria & Albert Museum. Crown Copyright.

MASTERPIECES
OF
QUEEN ANNE
&
GEORGIAN
FURNITURE

BY
F. LEWIS HINCKLEY

WITH 157 ILLUSTRATIONS

A WASHINGTON MEWS BOOK
Washington Square, New York

Other books by F. Lewis Hinckley

Directory of the Historic Cabinet Woods

Directory of Queen Anne, Early Georgian & Chippendale Furniture: Establishing the Preeminence of the Dublin Craftsmen

Hepplewhite, Sheraton & Regency Furniture

Queen Anne & Georgian Looking Glasses

Metropolitan Furniture of the Georgian Years

Library of Congress Cataloging-in-Publication Data

Hinckley, F. Lewis.
   Masterpieces of Queen Anne & Georgian furniture / by F. Lewis
Hinckley.
      p.   cm.
   ISBN 0-8147-3471-5
   1. Furniture, Queen Anne—Ireland—Dublin. 2. Furniture, Geor-
gian—Ireland—Dublin. 3. Furniture—Ireland—Dublin—Expertising. I.
Title. II. Title: Masterpieces of Queen Anne and Georgian furniture.
NK2538.D8H557 1991
749.22'91835'09033—dc20   90-43892
                                       CIP

Contents

Foreword

LEADING WRITERS on the subject have agreed that English furniture was made principally for royalty and the nobility and as a result very little is extant. Although their researches may not have extended so far back, their opinions are fully substantiated in the collectors' magazines that were published during the turn of the nineteenth century. In these the advertisements of London antique dealers offer their importations of Dutch, Italian, French, and other Continental furniture, but little or nothing that can be recognized as English. Occasional examples of Irish-Chippendale pieces attest to the fact that a few owners of old Irish residences were then parting with the least attractive of their furnishings.

Through the undeniable evidence of those early photographic illustrations it is also obvious why members of the British aristocracy, from their awareness of that absence of high-quality Queen Anne and Georgian furniture in the London antique market, had already turned to Dublin for their furnishing or refurbishing needs. Thus in acquiring a Chippendale ribband-back settee and six chairs for Nostel Priory in about 1883,[1] Lord St. Oswald must have obtained these in Dublin, rather than London. Also, we now know that Lady Randolph Churchill during her Ireland years (1877-1881) was able to obtain choice pieces from ancestral homes in her rounds of the Dublin antique shops.[2]

The continued absence of fine Queen Anne and Georgian furniture in London during the later decades of the nineteenth century kept American antique dealers and interior decorators away from that market until about 1903. It was in that year that Daniel Farr found he could obtain the same high-quality (Dublin) merchandise in London under more comfortable circumstances. As owner of a most successful New York City antique shop, he (and his wealthy clientele) could well afford the one extra profit exacted by this easy change in his itinerary.

When English antique dealers joined those from the United States in patronizing the Dublin market and sometimes in also dealing directly with owners of old Irish residences, the same magazine advertisements show a gradually increasing panorama of distinctive Dublin seat furniture, cabinetwork, and looking glasses. Also, from 1905 on there was a steady increase of publications in book form, dealing with the subject of so-called Old English Furniture. These were routinely illustrated with the earliest Dublin imports to have arrived in England, some even prior to the 1900s, and then with many others as they continued arriving throughout the succeeding decades of the present century.

All such masterpieces received in London and New York during the last hundred years have been capital-city productions of which there are no London counterparts. Nevertheless, all have been arbitrarily accepted by museum and literary authorities as *English*, that is, as having been designed and executed in some nonexistent metropolitan furniture center of the Midlands, the North Country or some other English provincial area outside of London.

In contrast, every bona fide London production has always been recognized and acknowledged as such in all leading British and American museums and publications. In that regard it will be noticed that even to this day LONDON labels are extremely scarce in museum exhibits of Queen Anne and Georgian furniture and looking glasses, especially in comparison with those of the more numerous unrecognized Dublin masterpieces that are, and always have been, mistakenly labeled as ENGLISH.

The relatively small number of genuine London examples, in comparison with those of the more productive sister capital, also agrees with the observations of Parisian authorities who have drawn attention to the very few known former London cabinetmakers and joiners vis-à-vis the far greater number of known Parisian *ébénistes* and *menuisiers* who were registered in their officially regulated city guilds. Those particular differences will remain constant despite any possible further attempts to increase the number of London furniture makers[3] through publishing the names and street addresses of unknown woodworkers indiscriminately gleaned from their listings in old London Directorys.

As to documentary evidence, pedigrees such as those accompanying the relatively few important London productions that have been permitted to reach the public market, have but seldom accompanied the innumerable transfers of ancestral pieces that have been removed from old Irish castles and mansions throughout the last hundred years. Such omissions are attributable mainly to the fact that generations of American and English traders, in keeping with sound business practice, have refrained from voluntarily disclosing their private and/or commercial sources of supply.

---

[1] Edwards and Jourdain. *Georgian Cabinet-Makers.* London, 1955, p. 70.
[2] Ralph G. Martin. *Jennie*, Vol. 1. London, 1969.
[3] Sir Ambrose Heal. *The London Furniture Makers, 1660-1840.* London, 1953.

Queen Anne
and Georgian Furniture

Q UEEN ANNE AND GEORGIAN furniture of fine metropolitan designs was produced solely in one or the other of the two great British capitals: either in London as the second-largest city of the Western world, or in Dublin, third in size as well as in commercial and social importance during the seventeenth and eighteenth centuries. There were no other metropolitan furniture-producing centers in either country.

Nevertheless, except for a relatively small number of easily identifiable London productions made for royalty and the aristocracy in England, Scotland, and Wales, all other fine and equally distinctive Queen Anne and Georgian masterpieces have been misrepresented as *English* ever since the collecting of such antiques first came into vogue during the later decades of the nineteenth century; that is, as having originated in some undeterminable secondary furniture center supposedly existing somewhere within the English provinces as a whole. Thus hundreds of thoroughly characteristic masterpieces of Dublin furniture and looking glasses are now exhibited as *English* in all leading British and American museums and in illustrations appearing throughout the literature on so-called Old English Furniture.

The most important findings of R. W. Symonds, a former leading authority on that subject, appear to have been totally ignored by his large private and institutional followings. Through searches made of Irish shipping records he had learned that no evidence can be found of any English furniture ever having been received in that country prior to the Machine Age. He also stated, apparently after finally learning about the long existing Dublin trade, that any Queen Anne or Georgian furniture "known to have come out of Ireland is accepted as having been made there." However, this enlightenment came too late in his career for him to revise any of his many mistaken identifications, had he ever become aware of Dublin's importance as the major source of his *English furniture* (*vide* pls. 3, 20, 24-25), and had he ever become able and willing to make any such revisions.

Some of the less distinguished pieces that were illustrated by Symonds he assigned to the English North Country. The only antique furniture worthy of any consideration that is actually known to have originated in that area was produced by the much touted Gillow factory in Lancaster. Thus that little provincial town, with a population of 9,030 reached in the nineteenth century, became the second and only other furniture center to develop in England during the eighteenth century.

Aside from some pieces stamped with the name of that factory, other English (i.e.

provincial) furniture may occasionally be identified through the appearance of originally applied paper labels imprinted with the names and addresses of makers. Otherwise such provincial examples are generally so plain and indistinguishable in their designs as to be unworthy of illustrating either for advertising or educational purposes.

Dublin examples may also retain paper labels; while Dublin furniture is sometimes stamped with makers initials, rarely, with names (*vide* pls. 13, 17). Metal labels were never used in connection with any Queen Anne or Georgian furniture, despite the naive acceptance of such obviously manufactured evidence in respect to the so-called Channon Pieces.

The large number of chairs, settees, side tables, and so on, differing in various respects from the usual metropolitan examples, have seemed to indicate the possibility of a common Irish origin. Further comparative studies were therefore directed toward such productions, including those displaying extraordinary treatments that led to their being recognized, even during the early 1900s, as Irish-Chippendale examples. As a result it has finally been accepted that they do in fact comprise a subsidiary group of Dublin designs.

The grooved or deeply cleft knees of the wing chair (Ill. 7), the straddle chair (Ill. 8), and even of the fine architectural highboy selected for the Frontispiece, are one of the outstandingly characteristic features of that subsidiary class of Dublin furniture. The highboy, in which the handles and escutcheons are of a pattern also appearing on Philadelphia highboys, is illustrated in the *Dictionary of English Furniture* as a "Walnut Chest of Drawers on Stand, c. 1715" . . . a date some years prior to its actual Dublin production. In lieu of the ivory talons an undercutting of the claws was duplicated in equally fine and distinctive American work. One such instance is a Chippendale mahogany tray-top tea table authenticated as having been made by John Townsend of Newport, Rhode Island, *circa* 1765. Other similarly treated tea tables are recorded as made by John Goddard of Newport.

Documentations of Dublin's influence on the designing of Early American furniture also appear in the favor extended here to the trifid or drake foot (Ills. 15, 33, 34, 139), and also the faceted, petaled, or stockinged foot, as adopted in Philadelphia (Ill. 2 and 36), neither of which can be seriously considered as London innovations. Then, in addition to the distinctive shapings of chair frames, arms, arm supports, shoe pieces, and so on, some American back splats could only have been copied directly from patterns brought over with them by joiners trained in Dublin, rather than London.

The whorled-together arm terminals and arm supports, as in the two-chair-back settee (Ill. 12) is an especially imaginative and identifying Dublin treatment that was never repeated in any other furniture center of the eighteenth or early nineteenth century.

The most elaborated openwork splats appear in Late Chippendale productions (Ill. 29-31), one set of which has been stamped "T H 1826."

To suggest a close relationship between the flat-arched frieze rails of side tables such as Illustrations 41 and 43 and the similarly arched rails of much smaller pieces such as the stools in Illustrations 33 and 34 may seem rather farfetched. Nevertheless, even so trivial a consideration has served in confirming both types of examples as having originated in Dublin rather than in any smaller outlying town. A former designation of the stool (Ill. 34) as *English* has had to be changed to *Irish*, but it will take some additional time before museum authorities recognize its Dublin rather than provincial origin.

Fanciful or even grotesque carvings are common to the more heavily enriched of these subsidiary designs, as in Illustrations 40-45. The use of Virginia walnut in any of such examples is also indicative of capital-city work, rather than any provincial use of this southern variety of lavender-tinted American black walnut (*Juglans nigra*) as delivered to Dublin.

A special magazine article by R. W. Symonds was devoted to *The Chair with a Shell Back* (*The Antique Collector*, October 1956), in which he illustrated an armchair matching the one here (Ill. 42) in order to emphasize the extravagent carving of some craftsmen in contrast to the more refined taste of others. He considered it "unusual for an English chair to suffer these defects" of eagle's heads and satyr masks. One of the examples he showed had been stamped with the initials "B R" surmounted by a crown. Other chairs that he illustrated were stamped with the initials "T.T." This he accepted as showing that shell-back chairs were made by not one but by several different firms of chairmakers . . . a combined Dublin production surely unheard of in respect to known London firms of the Georgian years.

Georgian decorated lacquer cabinets supported on baroque carved and gilded, or silvered, stands (*vide* Ill. 45) have for many years been mistakenly designated as Charles II or William III productions. Actually, they comprise another subsidiary class of Dublin furniture. That some were evolved simultaneously with the most typical of Irish-Chippendale side tables is indicated by the incorporation of similar eagle heads, spread eagles, satyr masks, and so forth in their stands. Late Chippendale effects are also present, most noticeably in an open-fret gallery with tiny ball finials, Plate 107 in my *Directory of Queen Anne, Early Georgian & Chippendale Furniture*. Further proof of this corrective information appears in the late methods of drawer construction employed in such cabinets.

Despite its description in the sale of the Rovensky Collection as a "Louis XV Kingwood Marquetry Commode Flemish or North German, XVIII Century," that piece (Ill. 46) is representative of a subsidiary quality of Dublin furniture. It does not approach the standard of excellence achieved in Dublin-Hepplewhite grand serpentine-bombé marquetry commodes. The drawers of equal depths are also edged and bordered in the French manner, while the placing of the keyholes indicates the use of square locks, rather than the long locks used by French cabinetmakers. Although the drawer linings are of mahogany, they and the pine carcase, as well as all exterior shapings, are poorly executed. Identification is therefore dependent on the distinctively inlaid Dublin marquetry panels in their scrolling branches of blossoms and foliations (obviously supplied by a more skilled artisan), plus the original, unmistakable Dublin ormolu handles, of a Late Chippendale pattern, which were also either delivered to, or copied by, one of the finest cabinetmakers working in Boston, Massachusetts, to enhance a fine bombé chest of drawers.

A number of shepherd's-crook armchairs have remained available to this latest research project as vividly displaying a wealth of other structural elements, overall forms, back and splat shapings, front and rear leg and foot treatments, carvings, and so on, all of which are as thoroughly typical of Dublin Queen Anne and Early Georgian designs as they are atypical of any designs that were actually produced in London (*vide* Ills. 54, 57, 60, 66, 67 and 69).

Considering the varieties of Spanish feet that are characteristic of both Dublin and American furniture, the one used in both the front and rear legs of the upholstered side chair (Ill. 63) is more pronounced than those in Illustration 62, but less so in comparison with those of the side table (Ill. 83). The gilded side chair in original Genoese velvet (Ill. 63) is recorded as having been made for Sir William Humphreys, the crest displaying his coat of arms. However, like many Dublin masterpieces so recorded, its obvious Dublin origin has not been mentioned. Rather, a London origin has been left to be assumed from Sir William's address in that capital and from the fact that he was Lord Mayor from 1714 to 1715.

Many such examples have been documented as being specially made for the British royal family and members of the nobility, with those documentations falling short of revealing the names and addresses of their Dublin makers. Should any American furniture of consequence be exhibited or published with attention being directed only to original ownerships and complete avoidance of the more enlightening information, this would certainly draw prompt and general disapproval.

In contrast, even though such information might be far more pertinent toward attaining a better understanding of London furniture, questions seem never to have been raised as to just why such makers' names and their Dublin addresses have so often been overlooked, ignored, lost, or withheld.

The pair of upholstered side chairs (Ills. 72-73) are part of an unusually large Dublin production of matching side and armchairs. Of these Percy Macquoid illustrated an armchair and side chair, Figs. 104-105 in his *Age of Mahogany.* One of those chairs had been applied with an advertisement that Macquoid considered an originally applied label of Giles Grendy, although no other such chair of that entire Dublin production had ever, or has ever, been found to have been similarly treated.

Eight matching side chairs from that same large production had been brought over from Ireland by Sir Spencer Ponsonby Fane when he, with his Irish bride and their family heirlooms, settled in Brympton D'Enercy, in Somerset. Every one of Sir Spencer's chairs was stamped with the initials W F—obviously those of their Dublin maker.

Apparently it has not seemed at all suspicious to English museum and literary authorities that of such an exceptionally large production only the one chair has ever turned up with such an obviously fraudulent advertisement. Instead, on that basis alone, they have attributed a wide variety of equally typical Dublin examples to Giles Grendy, including the clothes press (Ill. 89), although none has been similar in any way to the work he is actually known to have carried out. In contrast, antique dealers have shown much greater discipline in handling such pieces, not claiming Grendy as the maker even of such chairs as those that are so authoritatively illustrated in the *Age of Mahogany.*

Also contrasting with such professional discipline is the now customary disregard of statements made by Pierre Langlois in his authentic trade label. He did not lay claim to being a *marqueteur,* as he has so glibly been misrepresented by English museum and literary authorities. Instead, he plainly and unequivocally stated that he "inlaid in the politest manner with brass and tortoiseshell." In other words he specialized in *boullework,* which cannot possibly be construed according to the accepted understanding of marquetry or marquetry work.

Langlois had returned to France by the time he was about thirty-five years old, or *circa* 1770—too early to lend credence to the multiplying claims that he made all or any of the Dublin grand serpentine-bombé marquetry commodes now so blindly associated with his name.

The bureau dressing table as a favorite Dublin form was fashioned in various interpretations of William and Mary, Queen Anne, and Early Georgian designs. The restrained shaping and molding of the flat-arched mirror frame surmounting the present example (Ill. 85) were duplicated in many dressing mirrors that were supported on shallow plateaus of small drawers. Some of those received in Philadelphia were labeled by John Elliott, their source left to be mistakenly inferred from his newspaper advertisements calling attention to various "looking glasses just arrived in ships from London." Others received there were labeled by Wayne and Biddle as successors to James Stokes.

As wholesale as well as retail dealers, the Elliotts could not have afforded to buy their looking glasses in the London market. Only the wealthiest Britishers would have been able to afford the costs there, which would have had to include the exorbitant excise taxes that were levied on all types of English glasswares.

The fact that Irish glass of every description was obtainable tax-free in that country accounts also for the huge shipments of Waterford glasswares received in America. These of course included Waterford chandelieres, such as those still hanging in many English great houses, as well as in Trinity Church, New York, and Independence Hall, Philadelphia. It also accounts for all of the really consequential wall mirrors of ever-varying Queen Anne, Early Georgian, Chippendale, and Later Georgian designs that were shipped from Dublin to Philadelphia, Boston, and New York during the eighteenth century.

In the study of such veneered walnut examples, the most important features of the bureau (Ill. 84) are either entirely or partially concealed. Though exhibited as *Dutch* it could not have been made in that country, since the veneers are laid on pine instead of the hardwood cores that were mandatory in Holland. The other most decisive features are the handles and the escutcheon, which have been helpful in confirming other early Dublin designs, in particular through a full-size pattern made of the escutcheon.

Clues that were helpful at the start of these particular researches are obvious in the illustration of the secretaire (Ill. 92). The coved stellate inlay in particular was most significant, then the particular type of arched pediment with flaming-urn finials, and later the distinctive patterns of the escutcheons and handles. It soon became clear that its former designation as *English* was not only misleading in respect to origin, but was also a great disparagement of its prestigious capital-city status.

It had seemed likely that this particular secretaire would be schematically linked to another of a varying design that also embodied the same type of coved stellate or sunburst inlay. This appeared in an early *Country Life* advertisement as one of the pieces to be sold from the original contents of an important old Welsh residence. It seemed only logical that these handsome furnishings would have been obtained directly from Dublin, so conveniently situated just across the St. George's Channel, rather than having to be ordered in, and then be delivered from, the faraway English capital. Eventually this proved to be the case, and all such recessed inlays appearing in other walnut or mahogany case pieces of related designs have invariably served in confirming their true Dublin origins.

The side chair (Ill. 109) is one of a set of twelve from Bramshill Park, Hampshire. Matching chairs and chair-back settees have been illustrated by R. W. Symonds as coming from the same collection, and also from Shire End, Perthshire, Scotland. As the principal eulogist of unrecognized Dublin seat furniture and cabinetwork he declared that "The high grade of execution of the carving and the graceful contour of the backs unquestionably signify the skilled craftsmanship of the London chair-maker; one of high standing in the trade with many customers both in town and country."

Years ago a Chinese-Chippendale side chair matching the armchair (Ill. 118) was published as "From Simpson's Hospital, an old Dublin Foundation." Percy Macquoid (*Age of Mahogany*, Fig. 14) published another with eagle-head arm terminals. Other coincidences such as these, and the fact that many chairs of related designs have appeared in Scottish collections and in Scottish dealers' advertisements, first suggested the then surprising possibility of Dublin as their source.

When this had been firmly established as a reality a still further problem remained. This had resulted from a noticeable lack of aging in some Chippendale productions, compared with the usual degrees of patination and oxidation commonly found in others. For instance, some dealers could not accept the armchair (Ill. 118) as an eighteenth century example, while others found it barely acceptable in that light.

Those appreciable differences in aging were finally explained through a report concerning a three-tier circular tripod dumbwaiter similar to the one here (Ill. 129), but which was surmounted by a Regency ormolu gallery. In the revised edition of the *Dictionary of English Furniture* this had been dated as *circa* 1760, and it was noted as bearing a trade label of *Mack, Williams, and Gibton, 39 Stafford Street*. As such an address was not to be found in London, it was left to be assumed that it must have referred to some other (nonexistent) metropolitan furniture producing center elsewhere in England. A report from Dublin explained the impossibility of the 1760 *circa* date, since the piece had actually been made more than fifty years later.

Other Late Chippendale pieces, such as the octagonal cellarettes in Illustrations 131-132, have also been illustrated by English literary authorities with incorrect *circa* dates. Thus the one with inlaid cover appears in the literature as a pre-Chippendale example of *circa* 1740! The brass-bound example with typical Chippendale legs and C-brackets could not have been made any earlier than the turn of the eighteenth century. It is fitted with an original machine-made lever lock as then first being introduced in London, and then delivered to Dublin—as indicated by the small round escutcheon plate.

Although generally associated with Sheraton tables of various forms and sizes, the original triple reeding of the table edge in Illustration 136 is not a mid-century treatment, and therefore this particular drop-leaf dining table is better described as Georgian, or George III, rather than George I, as it was formerly designated.

The long-continued popularity of Chippendale designs in Dublin was especially noticeable in the lack of aging, particularly in respect to the interior surfaces, of the library table (Ill. 144). In this the original handles of a typical Late Chippendale pattern later served as corroborative evidence, not only for the piece itself, but far more importantly, toward helping to point out and finally clear up the carelessly accepted Channon Hoax.

The Channon Hoax

The ormolu-mounted mahogany serpentine-front commode in Illustration 145 is the most reserved of three such museum acquisitions that have been unthinkingly claimed for a provincially trained craftsman, the most lavish of which was purchased by the Victoria and Albert Museum for "£5,000 with the help of a substantial grant from the National Collections Fund with a contribution from Messrs. H. Blairmann and Sons." This is illustrated in my *Metropolitan Furniture of the Georgian Years*, Ill. 22; its central drawers feature handles of a Late Chippendale pattern appearing in the inset accompanying the Late Chippendale library table (Ill. 144 here), with all handles of the same pattern.

A London working address had been unearthed for a provincially trained craftsman, one John Channon, to whom those three acquisitions and an equally unmistakable Dublin rosewood chair, with whorled-together arm terminals and arm supports, had been attributed. Those museum attributions had been made on the basis of two unattractive, especially cumbersome bookcases at Powderham Castle. According to a *Victoria & Albert Bulletin* for April 1966, "Each of these is signed [sic] and dated on a brass plaque set in the middle of the door frame at the bottom. The signature [sic] J. CHANNON is in Gothic lettering and is accompanied by the date 1740."

Unfortunately, the most elementary research had not been carried out, for the Powderham bookcases had already been examined and reported on by Ralph Edwards and Margaret Jourdain years before. In *Georgian Cabinet-Makers* they had recorded that "T. CHANNON fecit is inscribed on a brass plate attached to one (NB) of a pair of . . . bookcases at Powderham Castle."

Clearly, then, that single unorthodox metal plate that had been attached to one bookcase had been removed from the piece. It must then have been replaced by a newer brass plate, together with another added brass plate, and in both instances these had been engraved to order with the name: "J. CHANNON," not followed by "fecit," but instead followed by the date 1740 after which the two newer brass plates had been set in the middle of each door frame at the bottom.

The leading English authority, R. W. Symonds, wrote a special article for the *Leeds Museum Art Calendar* (No. 39) on the commode acquired for Temple Newsam, which is similar to the one here (Ill. 145), except that it has brass-inlaid borders around the top edge and at the base. In that article he described the museum's Dublin masterpiece as "AN ENGLISH COMMODE OF A RARE DESIGN AND QUALITY" one of "three most important pieces of English furniture to have come to light within the last eight years. . . . In 1956 it appeared on the London antique market. . . . The quality of the cabinet work was of the same high order and with the same English handwriting of the other two pieces. . . . The writing cabinet was sold to a collector in America, but as the English licensing authorities recognized its importance no export license was granted. It therefore remained in England. . . . When an even more important library table appeared it was immediately bought by the Victoria and Albert Museum, who realized the outstanding importance of this piece in the evolution of English cabinet work. . . . The third piece like the cabinet was never allowed to leave the country, and it now forms part of the important collection at Temple Newsam. . . . Students, therefore, and all others who are interested in English furniture, must be thankful that these three remarkable specimens of English furniture remain in the country of their origin. That they do so is undoubtedly because of the enlightened attitude and increased knowledge brought about by the more serious study given to English furniture in recent years. . . . The commode is unquestionably English in design . . . in the traditional English manner . . . English work . . . English taste . . . . The construction . . . denotes English work." *English ad infinitum* with no thought of the only English metropolitan furniture producing center as London, itself; and no idea that he was lavishing such praise on *Dublin* designs, *Dublin* quality, *Dublin* cabinet work, and so on.

A pair of such fine Dublin commodes with rococo handles possibly like, or somewhat like, the ones appearing in the Victoria and Albert library table, the Temple Newsam commode, and the one here (Ill. 145), is described by Edwards and Jourdain in *Georgian Cabinet-Makers*, p. 102: "Each of a pair of fine serpentine-fronted mahogany commodes, c. 1760, with elaborate brass rococo handles, formerly in the Samuel Courtauld Collection, bears the trade label of . . . MACK, WILLIAMS and GIBTON. They are described as 'Upholsterers and Cabinet Makers to His Majesty, His Excellency the Lord Lieutenant and the Rt. Hon. His Majesty's Board of Works, 39 Stratford [sic] Street, Dublin. N. B. Auctions, Valuations and Funerals Attended.'"

As leading researchists in the field of Georgian furniture, apparently neither author attempted to confirm their *circa* date of 1760 for that pair of commodes, or their *Fl. circa* 1760 as the height of their working period; this despite the obvious great success and importance of this royal sponsorship of a Dublin firm. Through failing to do so they apparently never became acquainted with the subject of Late Chippendale Furniture.

John Teahan, Keeper of the Art and Industrial Division, National Museum of Ireland, was kind enough to send me the following invaluable information: "John Mack, cabinet maker, had an address at 188 Abbey Street in 1785. In the period 1794-1800 he also had an address at 39 Stafford Street. Soon after this he began to work in partnership with another cabinet maker called Gibton and they were listed at the same addresses in 1805 and 1810. Around this time they were joined by another cabinet maker called Williams. Mack, Williams and Gibton were listed together at 39 Stafford Street from 1815 to 1825."

John Teahan's letter also contained information on one *Kearney, Carver, Gilder and Looking Glass Maker to His Majesty*, whose label appeared on the back of an architectural wall mirror of the distinctive Dublin type that English lay writers identify as *Early Georgian; vide* Oliver Brackett, *English Furniture, Illustrated*, 186. These notices of patronages extended by members of the royal family in London to craftsmen employed in Dublin may have some bearing on the latter capital's great furniture production vis-à-vis that of London. Therefore, any information about those to whom such patronages were extended may eventually prove useful. As a matter of fact, no such notice of a similar patronage having been conferred upon a single London master has ever been found on any of the thousands of pieces that have passed through my hands during the past fifty years. In the present instance it was ascertained that "Joshua Kearney, carver and gilder, had an address at 186 Great Britain Street, from 1795 to around 1805. He then moved to 49 Henry Street, where he remained until at least 1820."

I have been hesitant about assigning Late Chippendale dates to the Victoria and Albert Museum's so-called Channon library table, authoritatively claimed to have been "Made in London during the 1740s," and thus also to the two commodes with handles of the same distinctive Dublin rococo pattern, none of which can honestly be claimed as in any way resembling London designs or London work. That hesitancy has continued despite the fact that the kneehole drawers of the library table are fitted with handles of a more common Late Chippendale pattern (*vide* inset Pl. 74), while the larger side drawers are yoke-fronted, in keeping with the same innovative Late Chippendale mode.

As to the Temple Newsam commode, its own rococo handles vouch for its close relationship to both the library table and the Fitzwilliam Museum commode. The latter example (Ill. 145), however, in its even more restrained ornamentation, nevertheless provides a determining clue to the Late Chippendale date of its own origin, and thus that of the other two pieces as well. The plain serpentine front shaping of its top, with slowly rounded front corners, plus its inset, wide, convex edging, is characteristic of other Late Chippendale commodes with handles of more customary Dublin patterns. Thus the top, as a single constituent part of the entire design, provides a determining clue not only to the Late Chippendale origin of the commode itself, but along with its handles, escutcheons, and stile mounts, also serve in similarly dating the other two pieces as well.[1]

It should be stressed here that with the additional years occupied in perfecting the designing and technical skills represented in the Late Chippendale masterpieces illustrated in this and my other books, they have already achieved, and will continue to command, artistic and monetary appreciations equal to or far exceeding either Dublin or London Chippendale examples produced during the 1750s and 1760s.

To encourage the acceptance of a second unsuspected instance of inscriptive chicanery, possibly by the same hoaxer, an English furniture historian, without acknowledgement of the earlier fraudulent inscription of *T. CHANNON fecit*, accepted as trustworthy the succeeding *Victoria & Albert Bulletin* account, in which it is noted that "J. CHANNON is accompanied by the date 1740" in each of a pair of similarly fraudulent inscriptions. In his opening paragraph of a *Connoisseur* article of May 1971, "Some Weekes' Cabinets Reconsidered," Christopher Gilbert declared that:

> One of the most encouraging advances ever made in the study of English furniture flowed from the identification by R. W. Symonds of a small, well-defined group of mahogany cabinet-pieces displaying marked technical and stylistic similarities, one common feature being the use of brass inlay combined with luxurious ormolu mounts of distinctive rococo design. Publication of this group led to the discovery of further specimens and eventually[2] a sumptuous pair of rosewood bookcases, invested with the characteristic embellishments and bearing brass tablets inscribed "J. Channon Fecit 1749," was located at Powderham Castle, near Exeter, permitting attribution of the entire group to this firm. Following this triumph the evidence of stylistic analogy as a means of determining authorship was, perhaps inevitably, used a trifle rashly and the whole issue of Channon's workshop is currently being re-researched. The initial breakthrough was, nevertheless, a major achievement, and it is possible that this article will provide the stimulus for a similar success.

Just as there are no "marked technical and stylistic similarities" to be found between the typical Dublin extravaganzas so willfully associated with the name of a provincially indoctrinated craftsman, and any bona fide London productions, there will be no such similarities discoverable between the equally typical Dublin clock cabinets and any cabinets truthfully determinable as having been produced in London.

This will hold true not only in respect to the overall Dublin designs, varying astragal arrangements, panel inlays, basic valanced treatments, *pieds en toupie*, or other turned supports, but also in regard to the patterns of bail, and *ajouré* patera, and handles, as well as those of the ormolu galleries surmounting the smaller related, allied, or fringe pieces. In fact it is these particular decorative features and subordinate details that are especially characteristic of Dublin, rather than London, furniture.

Failure to recognize them as such can only detract from the authority and assumed expertise of English museum personnel. After all, no one can have a proper understanding of Queen Anne and Georgian furniture as a whole, while at the same time denying the very real presence of Dublin as the third-largest capital-city furniture center of the eighteenth century.

Despite the silver or other metal adjuncts that have been introduced in some of the Dublin clock cabinets, or those possibly featuring instead a jasperware medallion or convex mirror, these extrinsic items do not alter the fact that the cabinets themselves are of incontestable Dublin, rather than London, designs. Thus any continued meaningless search by Christopher Gilbert or his colleagues among the insignificant proportion of labeled or documented (London) furniture of the period must come to naught.

Furthermore, the inscription "Weekes Museum Titchborne Street," as added to the customary plain dials of the commonplace clocks in presently so-called *Weekes Cabinets*, was obviously added toward the promotion of a privately run, supposedly "renowned" and "celebrated" exhibition room where Thomas Weekes's relatively unimportant objects were shown, such as "mechanical curiosities, animated spiders and birds of paradise, ingenious clocks, musical instruments, elaborate temples and a wide range of expensive toys and contrivances."

That description gives additional credence to the thought previously expressed in these researches, that it would be most unlikely for any of the regular-sized Dublin clock cabinets to be displayed amid such a melange, either side by side, or more openly arranged in one room of such a small place, certainly not one formerly "renowned" or "celebrated" for dealing in such choice Dublin importations. An illustration of a thoroughly representative Dublin clock cabinet, in West Indian satinwood, thuja and sabicu, was contributed for my *Directory of the Historic Cabinet Woods* (p. 49) through the courtesy of H. Blairmann & Sons; *vide* there also pp. 6-9.

Many Dublin cabinets have been mistakenly attributed to Vile and Cobb, or William Vile, especially those featuring circular or oval panel moldings interrupted by leaf clasps or other types of foliations, supposedly resembling the carvings of pieces made by Vile for Buckingham Palace and Windsor Castle. In the instance of the rosewood veneered dwarf cabinet with gilded gesso panels and frieze (Ill. 147), having also been attributed to William Vile (Edwards and Jourdain, *Georgian Cabinet-Makers*, 1955, Pl. 57), this has passed even further beyond the bounds of reality. Vile never worked in either the late style or the medium of these applied gesso enrichments. This should have been obvious, since he died in 1767. The association is also meaningless in a judgment of value, for another such rosewood piece, but with marquetry rather than relief ornament and with its ormolu moldings clearly indicating a Dublin production of the late Georgian years, was sold for twenty-two thousand dollars, at auction, some years ago when that figure would represent the equivalent of eighty-eight thousand dollars in today's currency. *Vide* the *Dictionary of English Furniture*, Fig. 15.

With a special constructional method introduced by Dublin craftsmen in the making of double-doored cabinets, framings of the glass panels are reciprocally chamferred so that they meet in a central overlap (*vide* Ills. 150 and 154). This of course permits a fuller display of the contents than when glazed doors meet in the usual manner.

The only multifold screens represented in these research files are those that, uniformly hinged and bordered in gilded leather, are painted on leather with soft rich colors in gold-scale grounds, with genre or pastoral scenes, supposedly copied from pictures by Lancret and other French artists. Resemblances to pictures painted by Irish artists or to scenes worked in Irish needlepoint seem never to have been noticed by English authorities. Nor have any likenesses been observed in the country scenes with farm animals, thatched cottages, and so on, that appear in the églomisé panels of Dublin wall mirrors. The low four-fold example (Ill. 157), is typical of those included in views of old Irish residences and may well have been one of those included in "a great Choice of guilt leather and painted screens" that was advertised in the *Dublin Journal* of August 29th, 1747.

---

[1] While these final determinations have been arrived at without examinations of the pieces to determine the actual amount of aging in comparison with that expectable in pieces really dating from the 1740s, when these Dublin importations are eventually examined by chosen members of the British Antique Dealers' Association, it will be found that in each of these three instances *Designs Speak For Themselves*, not only as to their true Dublin origins, but also as to their Late Chippendale dates of production.

[2] For Christopher Gilbert to say that publication of the so-called Channon library table and commodes led eventually to the discovery of a pair of bookcases bearing tablets inscribed J. Channon Fecit 1740, is quite the direct opposite of the procedure followed in carrying out the infamous Channon Hoax. The one Powderham bookcase had been tagged *J. Channon Fecit* many years before its single tag had been removed in favor of two tags each with the date *1740* added, as "discovered" by the writer of the *Victoria & Albert Museum Bulletin* article of April 1966. To say that the Powderham bookcases *eventually*, rather than formerly, appeared, as falsified evidence in the Channon Hoax, is not accurate museum reportage, to put it mildly.

Notes and References Re Some Illustrated Examples

Ill. 12. Ring-collared cabriole legs, as here, have long been noted by English authorities as characteristic of Irish seat furniture.

Ills. 17-18. The popular Dublin corner chair with high back in two stages is an innovation that was sparingly introduced in American seat furniture.

Ills. 21-22. The habitual volunteering of nonessential *circa* dates, as "*circa* 1760" for Late Chippendale designs such as Illustration 22, has resulted in errors of a half century or more; whereas a pre-Chippendale date of *circa* 1740 for a design such as that of Illustration 21, can be just as erroneous, given Dublin's retention of Early Georgian basic forms.

Ills. 23-24. Both Gothic-Chippendale side chairs showed aging commensurate only with examples dating from *circa* 1810-1830; or as the more characteristically Late Chippendale corner chair, Illustration 27. In the one shown at an angle, Illustration 24, the claw feet have been undercut, a rare treatment in Dublin as well as in Newport furniture.

Ill. 42. *Vide* the same back design in a Dublin walnut three-chairback settee, Fig. 112 in Percy Macquoid, *Age of Mahogany*.

Ill. 46. Handles of the same Late Chippendale pattern appear on a Late Chippendale mahogany clothes press, Fig. 140 in the *Age of Mahogany*; and on a Late Chippendale mahogany cupboard, with drawers in the center, optimistically dated as *circa* 1765 in the *Dictionary of English Furniture*.

Ills. 62-63. English authorities have never recognized the special orders that were filled in Dublin for seat furniture, cabinetworks, and the frames of looking glasses that were carved, inlaid, or otherwise embellished with monograms, coats-of-arms, or other heraldic devices for members of the aristocracy.

Ill. 69. An exactly matching armchair except for its veneers of burl ash, and not dating back into the same Early Georgian years, accompanied this walnut example in the sale of the Wadsworth Lewis Collection. Nevertheless, each chair brought the same price of $3,100, at the time when that figure was commensurate with some $12,000 today.

Ill. 70. An unusual Dublin example in no single feature resembling London work, and costing about $6,000 when that figure was equal to some $24,000 today.

Ill. 95. The same or an exactly matching "French" armchair was published by Constance Simon, *English Furniture Designers of the Eighteenth Century* (1905). It is apparent that like Percy Macquoid, she too had access to nineteenth-century Dublin importations then more abundantly entering the London antique market.

Ills. 96-97. Both featuring the cabochon arm terminals.

Ill. 104. Cf. the similarly carved seat edging, Fig. 113 in the *Age of Mahogany*.

Ill. 126. Gloucestershire has often been stressed in the present researches since, beginning with Badminton House, so many of the masterpieces that have been mistakenly attributed to Chippendale or other London makers have actually originated, instead, in the far more conveniently located Irish capital.

Ill. 138. Inversive gadrooning was one of several unconventional treatments that, while obviously acceptable in some Dublin shops, would have been quite unlikely to meet with approval in those of London.

Ill. 145. *Vide* the same rococo handles on a Rosewood chest of drawers, Fig. 128 in *Age of Mahogany*, also featuring Scandinavian-type openmouth escutcheons.

Ill. 146. *Vide* the same bail handles in Edwards and Jourdain, *Georgian Cabinet-Makers*, Pl. 94, a "Commode Clothes-Press, carved mahogany, *circa* 1755, Attributed to Thomas Chippendale. From a design in the *Director* (1st Edition) dated 1753."

Plates

PLATE 1

1 EARLY GEORGIAN WALNUT ARMCHAIR. Cf. feet of Ill. 37, arms of Ills. 2, 15, and 16.

2 EARLY GEORGIAN WALNUT ARMCHAIR. With faceted pad feet and flaring scrolled arm terminals as introduced in America. Courtesy of Needham's Antiques, Inc., New York City.

3 EARLY GEORGIAN WALNUT SIDE CHAIR. The shaped back uprights copied in New York.

4 EARLY GEORGIAN MAHOGANY SIDE CHAIR. Also with distinctively shaped back uprights. Cf. Ill. 68.

PLATE 2

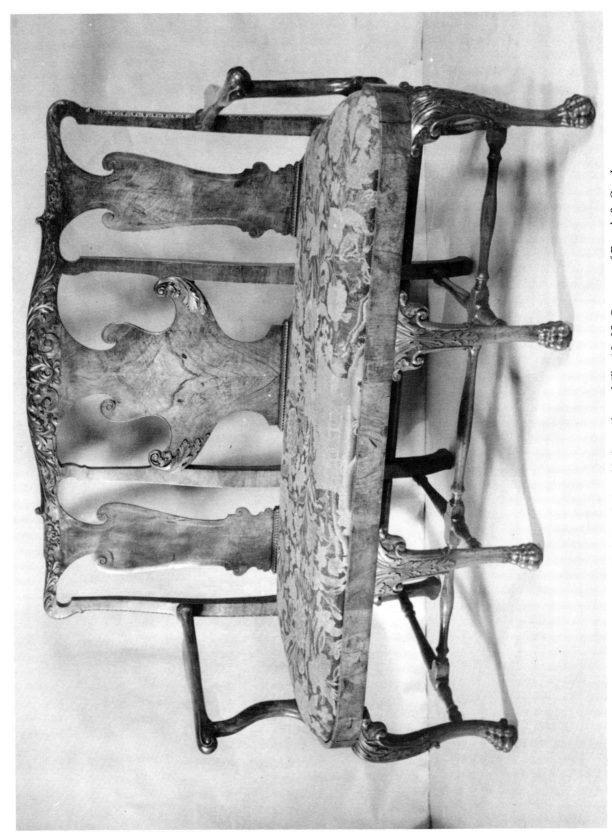

5   EARLY GEORGIAN WALNUT CHAIR-BACK SETTEE. With heavily knuckled paw feet; cf. Ills. 13, 35. Courtesy of French & Co., Inc., New York City.

PLATE 3

6   EARLY GEORGIAN WALNUT WING CHAIR. With distictive knee treatment and feet.

7   EARLY GEORGIAN WALNUT WING CHAIR. With distinctive knee treatment and rear feet.

PLATE 4

8 EARLY GEORGIAN MAHOGANY STRADDLE CHAIR.

9 EARLY GEORGIAN MAHOGANY ARMCHAIR.

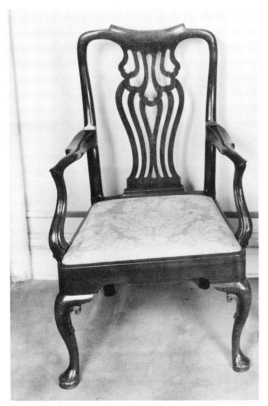

10 EARLY GEORGIAN MAHOGANY ARMCHAIR.
Courtesy of Needham's Antiques, Inc., New York City.

11 EARLY GEORGIAN MAHOGANY SIDE CHAIR.
Exported to the West Indies, as also the Late
Chippendale tripod table, Ill. 130. Courtesy of Tyge
Hvass, author of *Mobler Fra Dansk Vestindien.*

PLATE 5

12 EARLY GEORGIAN WALNUT CHAIR-BACK SETTEE.

13 EARLY GEORGIAN MAHOGANY CHAIR-BACK SETTEE. Cf. feet of Ill. 35.

PLATE 6

14 EARLY GEORGIAN MAHOGANY CORNER CHAIR. Cf. feet with Ill. 16.

15 EARLY GEORGIAN MAHOGANY UPHOLSTERED OPEN-ARM EASY CHAIR. Courtesy of J. J. Wolff (Antiques) Ltd., New York City.

PLATE 7

16   EARLY GEORGIAN WALNUT UPHOLSTERED OPEN-ARM SETTEE. Cf. Feet with Ill. 14, arms with Ill. 15. Metropolitan Museum of Art.

PLATE 8

17 EARLY GEORGIAN MAHOGANY HIGHBACK CORNER CHAIR.

18 EARLY GEORGIAN MAHOGANY HIGHBACK CORNER CHAIR.

PLATE 9

19 EARLY GEORGIAN CARVED AND TURNED WALNUT
TASSEL-BACK ARMCHAIR. Courtesy of French &
Company, Inc., New York City.

20 EARLY GEORGIAN WALNUT TASSEL-BACK CHAIR
WITH EAGLE-HEAD ARM TERMINALS.

PLATE 10

21 EARLY GEORGIAN MAHOGANY ARMCHAIR. With splat matching that of the following Late Chippendale example.

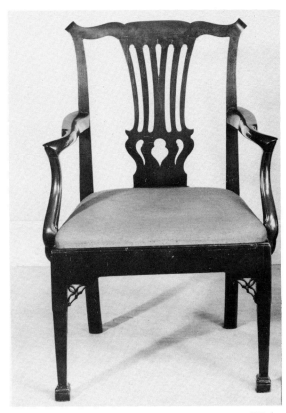

22 LATE CHIPPENDALE MAHOGANY ARMCHAIR. With characteristic arm and leg treatments and open-fret brackets.

23 LATE CHIPPENDALE MAHOGANY SIDE CHAIR. Cf. back splat with that of Ill. 27.

24 LATE CHIPPENDALE MAHOGANY SIDE CHAIR.

PLATE 11

25 LATE CHIPPENDALE MAHOGANY SIDE CHAIR.

26 LATE CHIPPENDALE MAHOGANY ARMCHAIR.

27 LATE CHIPPENDALE MAHOGANY CORNER CHAIR.

28 LATE CHIPPENDALE MAHOGANY LADDER-BACK
ARMCHAIR.

PLATE 12

29 LATE CHIPPENDALE MAHOGANY ARMCHAIR.

30 LATE CHIPPENDALE MAHOGANY SIDE CHAIR.

31 LATE CHIPPENDALE MAHOGANY SIDE CHAIR.

32 CHIPPENDALE MAHOGANY UPHOLSTERED OPEN-ARM
EASY CHAIR.

PLATE 13

33 EARLY GEORGIAN MAHOGANY WINE STAND.

34 EARLY GEORGIAN MAHOGANY STOOL. Victoria & Albert Museum. Crown Copyright.

35 EARLY GEORGIAN MAHOGANY WINE STAND. Cf. feet of Ills. 5, 13 and 37. Courtesy of Needham's Antiques, Inc., New York City.

PLATE 14

36 EARLY GEORGIAN MAHOGANY TRIANGULAR DROP-LEAF TABLE. With faceted or "stockinged" feet. *Vide* Ill. 12.

37 EARLY GEORGIAN MAHOGANY TRAY-TOP TABLE. Cf. feet of Ills. 1, 35.

PLATE 15

38 EARLY GEORGIAN MAHOGANY CARD TABLE. Cf. rear feet of Ills. 7, 39.

39 EARLY GEORGIAN MAHOGANY DROP-LEAF CENTER TABLE.

PLATE 16

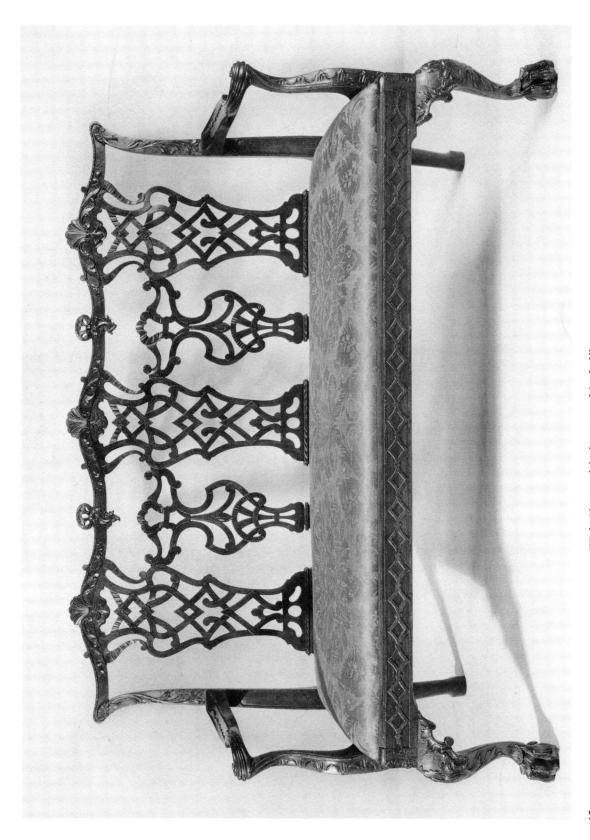

40   EARLY GEORGIAN MAHOGANY PAW-FOOT SETTEE. With Chippendale fret-pierced back filling.

PLATE 17

41 EARLY GEORGIAN PAW-FOOT SIDE TABLE. *En suite* with Ill. 40.

PLATE 18

42 EARLY GEORGIAN "SHELL-BACK" ARMCHAIR. Collection of
George F. Baker, New York City.

PLATE 19

43 EARLY GEORGIAN MAHOGANY SIDE TABLE.

PLATE 20

44 EARLY GEORGIAN MAHOGANY SIDE TABLE.

PLATE 21

45   GEORGIAN DECORATED LACQUER CABINET-ON-STAND. Victoria & Albert Museum. Crown Copyright.

PLATE 22

46 LATE LOUIS XV MARQUETRY COMMODE WITH ORIGINAL CHINESE-CHIPPENDALE HANDLES.

PLATE 23

47 QUEEN ANNE WALNUT CIRCULAR STOOL.

48 QUEEN ANNE WALNUT OVAL STOOL.

49 EARLY GEORGIAN WALNUT STOOL. With incurvate rails.

PLATE 24

50 EARLY GEORGIAN WALNUT STOOL.

51 EARLY GEORGIAN MAHOGANY STOOL.

52 EARLY GEORGIAN MAHOGANY STOOL.

53 EARLY GEORGIAN MAHOGANY STOOL. Collection of
J. P. Morgan, New York City.

PLATE 25

54 QUEEN ANNE WALNUT UPHOLSTERED ARMCHAIR.

55 QUEEN ANNE WALNUT UPHOLSTERED ARMCHAIR.

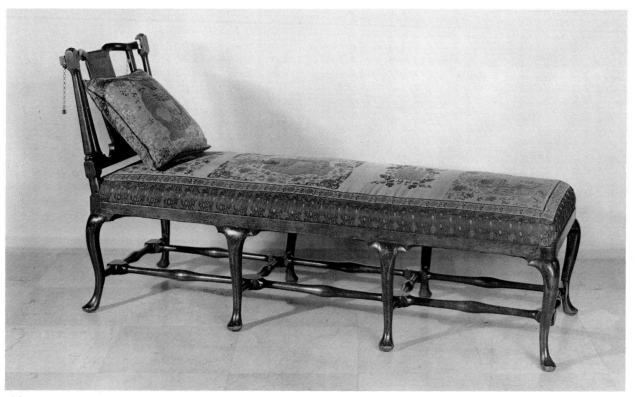

56 QUEEN ANNE WALNUT DAYBED.

PLATE 26

57 QUEEN ANNE WALNUT ARMCHAIR.

58 QUEEN ANNE WALNUT DAYBED.

PLATE 27

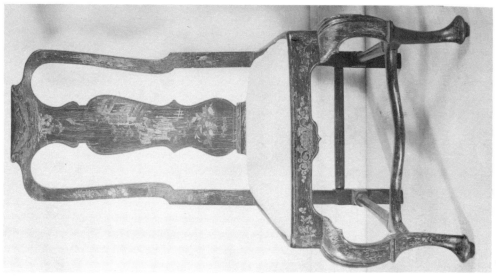

61 QUEEN ANNE DECORATED LACQUER SIDE CHAIR.

60 QUEEN ANNE WALNUT ARMCHAIR.

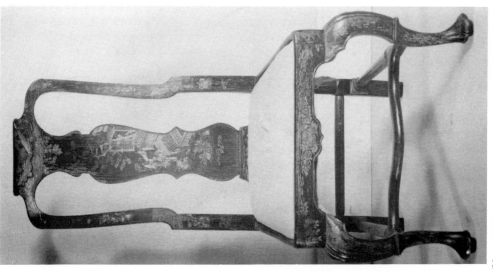

59 QUEEN ANNE DECORATED LACQUER SIDE CHAIR.

PLATE 28

62   QUEEN ANNE WALNUT UPHOLSTERED SETTEE WITH HERALDIC INLAYS.

PLATE 29

63   EARLY GEORGIAN GILDED SIDE CHAIR UPHOLSTERED IN GENOA VELVET. Victoria & Albert Museum.
Crown Copyright.

PLATE 30

64 EARLY GEORGIAN WALNUT SIDE CHAIR.

65 EARLY GEORGIAN WALNUT WING CHAIR *EN SUITE*.

PLATE 31

66 EARLY GEORGIAN CARVED AND INLAID WALNUT
ARMCHAIR. Victoria & Albert Museum.
Crown Copyright.

67 EARLY GEORGIAN WALNUT ARMCHAIR.

PLATE 32

68   EARLY GEORGIAN WALNUT SIDE CHAIR. Cf. back
uprights of Ill. 4.

69   EARLY GEORGIAN WALNUT ARMCHAIR WITH
COMPASS SEAT.

PLATE 33

70 EARLY GEORGIAN WALNUT UPHOLSTERED
ARMCHAIR.

71 EARLY GEORGIAN WALNUT UPHOLSTERED OPEN-
ARM CHAIR.

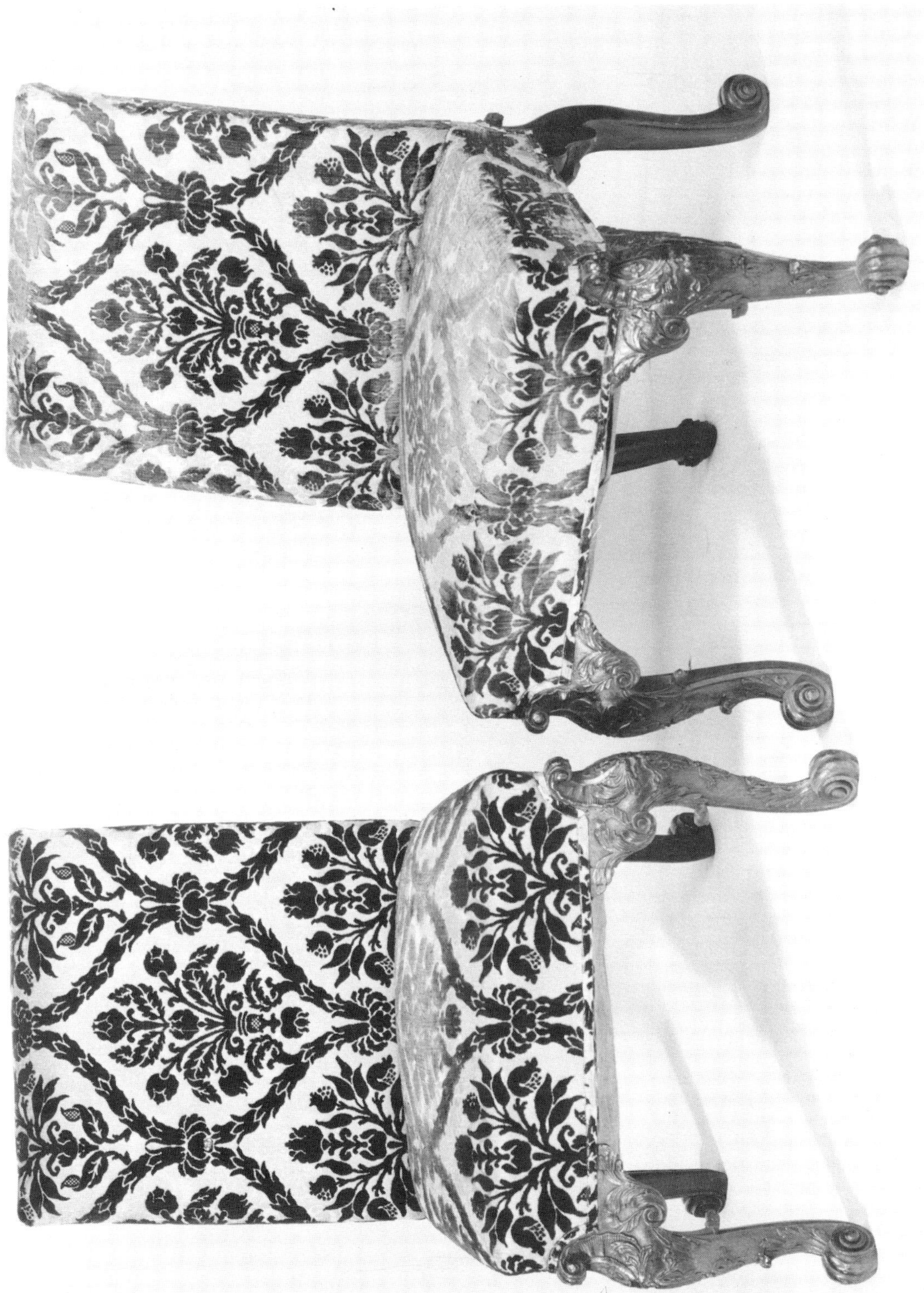

PLATE 34

72-73   PAIR EARLY GEORGIAN WALNUT UPHOLSTERED SIDE CHAIRS.

PLATE 35

74   EARLY GEORGIAN WALNUT UPHOLSTERED SETTEE.

PLATE 36

75 EARLY GEORGIAN WALNUT TASSEL-BACK SIDE CHAIR.

76 EARLY GEORGIAN MAHOGANY TASSEL-BACK SIDE CHAIR.

77 EARLY GEORGIAN WALNUT SIDE CHAIR.

78 EARLY GEORGIAN MAHOGANY ARMCHAIR.

PLATE 37

79 EARLY GEORGIAN CARVED AND INLAID MAHOGANY
CARD TABLE.

80 EARLY GEORGIAN CARVED MAHOGANY STOOL.

PLATE 38

81   EARLY GEORGIAN CARVED AND GILDED EAGLE CONSOLE.

82   EARLY GEORGIAN CARVED AND INLAID WALNUT SIDE TABLE.
With ormolu fittings of a distinctive Dublin pattern.

PLATE 39

83   EARLY GEORGIAN WALNUT SIDE TABLE. With Spanish feet as introduced in American furniture.

PLATE 40

84 QUEEN ANNE BUREAU-ON-STAND. Montreal Museum of Fine Arts.

85 EARLY GEORGIAN WALNUT BUREAU WITH DRESSING MIRROR.

PLATE 41

86   QUEEN ANNE INLAID WALNUT KNEEHOLE DESK.

PLATE 42

87   QUEEN ANNE INLAID WALNUT HIGHBOY.

PLATE 43

88   GEORGIAN INLAID WALNUT WRITING TABLE.

PLATE 44

89   EARLY GEORGIAN MAHOGANY CLOTHES PRESS. Victoria & Albert Museum. Crown Copyright.

PLATE 45

90 QUEEN ANNE INLAID WALNUT SECRETAIRE. Courtesy of French & Company, Inc., New York City.

PLATE 46

91   QUEEN ANNE INLAID WALNUT SECRETAIRE. Victoria & Albert Museum. Crown Copyright.

PLATE 47

92   EARLY GEORGIAN WALNUT SECRETAIRE WITH COVED STELLATE INLAY.

PLATE 48

93   EARLY GEORGIAN MAHOGANY SECRETAIRE WITH COVED STELLATE INLAY.

PLATE 49

94   EARLY GEORGIAN MAHOGANY ARCHITECTURAL SECRETAIRE. Handles changed.

PLATE 50

95 CHIPPENDALE ELABORATELY SHAPED AND CARVED *FRENCH CHAIR OF "DIRECTOR" DESIGN.*

96 CHIPPENDALE CARVED MAHOGANY UPHOLSTERED ARMCHAIR.

PLATE 51

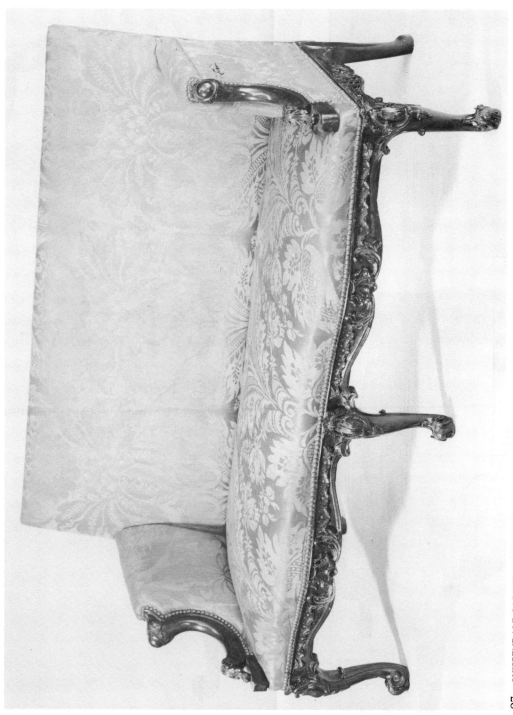

97 CHIPPENDALE CARVED MAHOGANY UPHOLSTERED SETTEE.

PLATE 52

98 CHIPPENDALE MAHOGANY UPHOLSTERED OPEN-ARM EASY CHAIR.

99 CHIPPENDALE MAHOGANY UPHOLSTERED OPEN-ARM EASY CHAIR.

PLATE 53

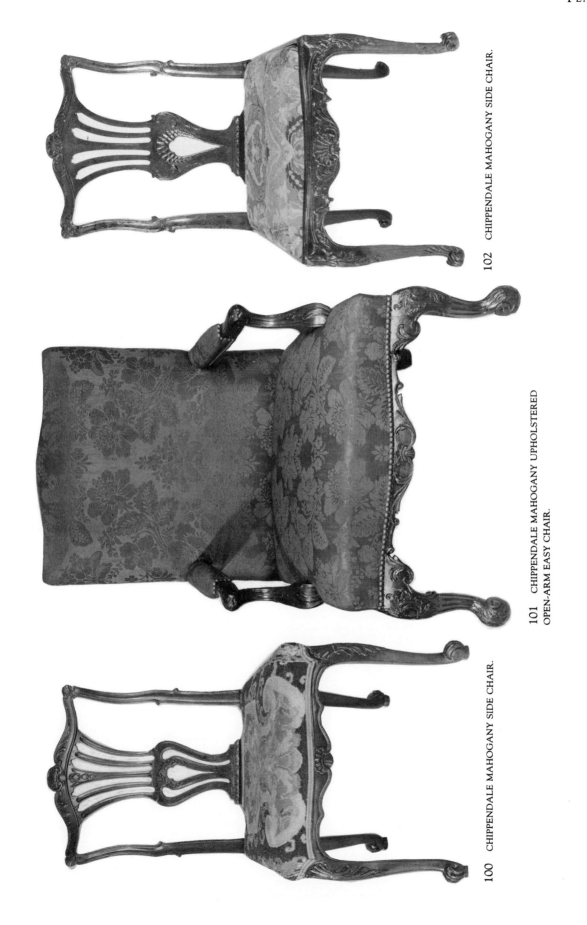

100 CHIPPENDALE MAHOGANY SIDE CHAIR.

101 CHIPPENDALE MAHOGANY UPHOLSTERED
OPEN-ARM EASY CHAIR.

102 CHIPPENDALE MAHOGANY SIDE CHAIR.

PLATE 54

103 CHIPPENDALE MAHOGANY UPHOLSTERED
OPEN-ARM EASY CHAIR.

104 CHIPPENDALE MAHOGANY RIBBAND-BACK SIDE
CHAIR. Cf. seat edging in Fig. 113, *Age of Mahogany*.
Victoria & Albert Museum. Crown Copyright.

PLATE 55

105 CHIPPENDALE MAHOGANY SIDE CHAIR.

106 CHIPPENDALE MAHOGANY RIBBAND-BACK SIDE
CHAIR. Cf. back treatment with that of Ill. 104.
Courtesy of J. J. Wolff (Antiques) Ltd., New York City.

PLATE 56

107 CHIPPENDALE MAHOGANY UPHOLSTERED
OPEN-ARM EASY CHAIR.

108 CHIPPENDALE MAHOGANY UPHOLSTERED
OPEN-ARM EASY CHAIR.

PLATE 57

109 CHIPPENDALE MAHOGANY SIDE CHAIR. From Bramshill Park, Hampshire. Courtesy of French & Company, Inc., New York City.

110 CHIPPENDALE MAHOGANY ARMCHAIR. Victoria & Albert Museum. Crown Copyright.

111 CHIPPENDALE MAHOGANY SIDE CHAIR.

112 CHIPPENDALE MAHOGANY ARMCHAIR.

PLATE 58

113 CHIPPENDALE MAHOGANY SIDE CHAIR.

114 CHIPPENDALE MAHOGANY SIDE CHAIR. Victoria & Albert Museum. Crown Copyright.

115 CHIPPENDALE MAHOGANY SIDE CHAIR. Courtesy of J. J. Wolff (Antiques) Ltd., New York City.

116 CHIPPENDALE MAHOGANY SIDE CHAIR. Cf. back of Ill. 42. Courtesy of J. J. Wolff (Antiques) Ltd., New York City.

PLATE 59

117   LATE CHIPPENDALE MAHOGANY ARMCHAIR.

118   LATE CHIPPENDALE MAHOGANY ARMCHAIR.

119   LATE CHIPPENDALE LABURNUM (?) ARMCHAIR.
Victoria & Albert Museum. Crown Copyright.

120   LATE CHIPPENDALE MAHOGANY ARMCHAIR.

PLATE 60

121 CHIPPENDALE MAHOGANY UPHOLSTERED
OPEN-ARM EASY CHAIR.

122 CHIPPENDALE MAHOGANY UPHOLSTERED EASY CHAIR.

PLATE 61

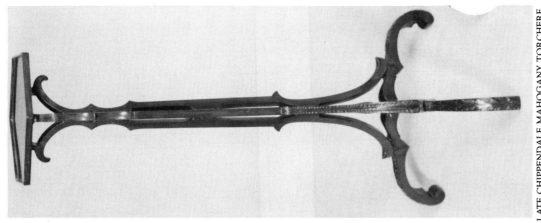

125   LATE CHIPPENDALE MAHOGANY TORCHERE.

124   CHIPPENDALE MAHOGANY BASIN STAND.

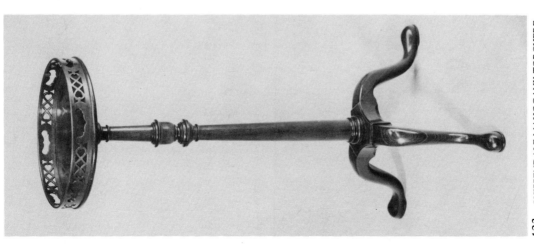

123   CHIPPENDALE MAHOGANY TORCHERE.

PLATE 62

126   CHIPPENDALE MAHOGANY TILTING-TOP TRIPOD TABLE. From Foster's Court Farm, near Gloucester. Victoria & Albert Museum. Crown Copyright.

PLATE 63

127   LATE CHIPPENDALE MAHOGANY TRAY-TOP TRIPOD TABLE. Victoria & Albert Museum. Crown Copyright.

PLATE 64

128   LATE CHIPPENDALE MAHOGANY TRAY-TOP TRIPOD TABLE.

129   LATE CHIPPENDALE MAHOGANY DUMBWAITER.

PLATE 65

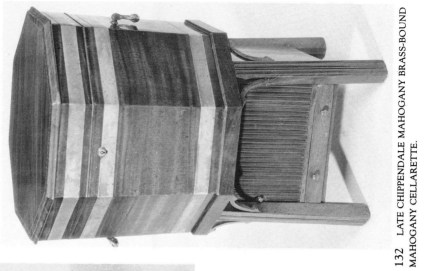

132 LATE CHIPPENDALE MAHOGANY BRASS-BOUND
MAHOGANY CELLARETTE.

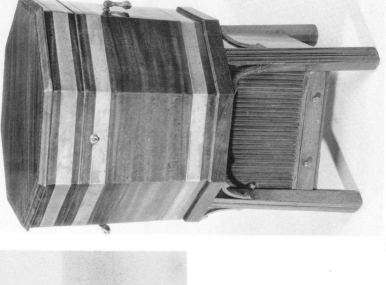

130 LATE CHIPPENDALE MAHOGANY TRIPOD TABLE.
Exported to the West Indies, as also the Georgian side
chair, Ill. 11. Courtesy of Tyge Hvass, author of
Mobler Fra Dansk Vestindien.

131 LATE CHIPPENDALE CARVED AND INLAID
MAHOGANY CELLARETTE.

PLATE 66

133   CHIPPENDALE MAHOGANY CENTER TABLE.

PLATE 67

134 LATE CHIPPENDALE FRET-
CARVED MAHOGANY SILVER TABLE.

135 LATE CHIPPENDALE FRET-CARVED MAHOGANY SILVER TABLE.

PLATE 68

136   GEORGIAN MAHOGANY DROP-LEAF DINING TABLE.

PLATE 69

137   CHIPPENDALE MAHOGANY ARCHITECTURAL WRITING TABLE.

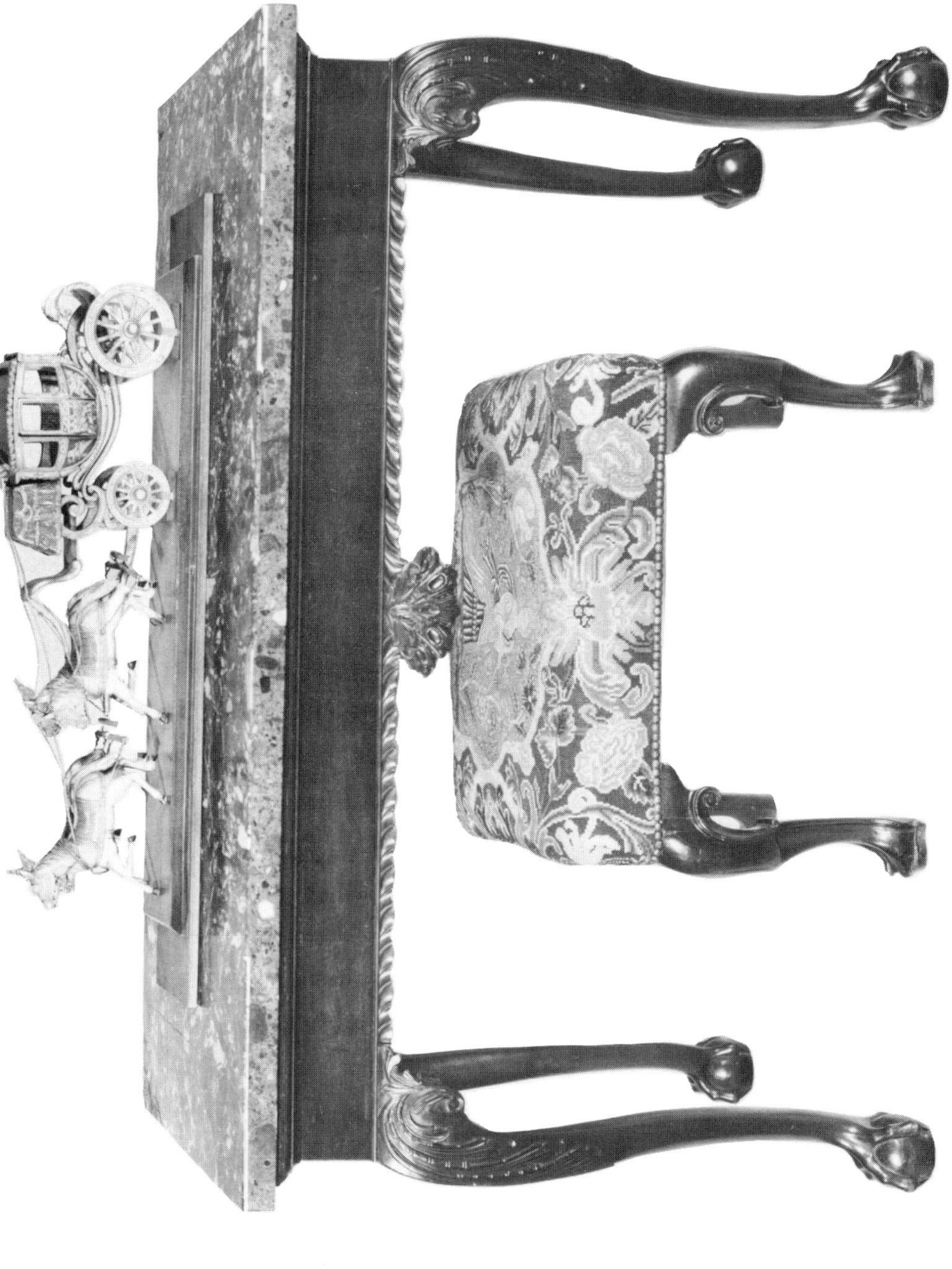

PLATE 70

138 CHIPPENDALE MAHOGANY SIDE TABLE. Courtesy of French & Company, Inc., New York City.

139 GEORGIAN WALNUT DRAKE-FOOT STOOL. Cf. feet of Ills. 15, 33, and 34.

PLATE 71

140 CHIPPENDALE MAHOGANY SERPENTINE-FRONT SIDE TABLE.

PLATE 72

141   ENTRANCE, KILKEA CASTLE, COUNTY KILDARE. Seat of the Marquis of Kildare.

90

PLATE 73

INTERIOR VIEW, KILKEA CASTLE.
142   CHIPPENDALE INLAID ROSEWOOD SERPENTINE-FRONT COMMODE, MOUNTED IN ORMOLU.
143   CHIPPENDALE PARCEL-GILDED SIDE CHAIR. Cf. Ill. 102.

PLATE 74

144 LATE CHIPPENDALE MAHOGANY LIBRARY TABLE.

PLATE 75

145   LATE CHIPPENDALE MAHOGANY SERPENTINE-FRONT COMMODE, MOUNTED IN ORMOLU. Reproduced by permission of the Syndics of the Fitzwilliam Museum, Cambridge, England.

PLATE 76

146 LATE CHIPPENDALE MAHOGANY SERPENTINE-FRONT COMMODE. With original bail handles of a favorite Dublin pattern. Courtesy of H. Douglas Curry, New York City.

PLATE 77

147 LATE CHIPPENDALE ROSEWOOD-VENEERED AND GILDED GESSO MEUBLE D'ENTREDEUX. Reproduced by permission of the Syndics of the Fitzwilliam Museum, Cambridge, England.

PLATE 78

148   CHIPPENDALE ROSEWOOD-VENEERED COLLECTOR'S CABINET ON CARVED MAHOGANY STAND.

PLATE 79

149 JAPANESE DECORATED LACQUER CABINET ON CONTEMPORARY LATE CHIPPENDALE CARVED, PAINTED AND
PARCEL-GILDED STAND. Victoria & Albert Museum. Crown Copyright.

PLATE 80

150   LATE CHIPPENDALE MAHOGANY DISPLAY CABINET.

PLATE 81

151   LATE CHIPPENDALE MAHOGANY HANGING SHELVES.

152   CHIPPENDALE MAHOGANY SECRETAIRE WITH
OPEN-FRET BOOK SHELVES. Courtesy of Trevor, Ltd.,
London.

PLATE 82

153 LATE CHIPPENDALE MAHOGANY ARCHITECTURAL PIER CABINET. Courtesy of French & Company, Inc.,
New York City.

PLATE 83

154   LATE CHIPPENDALE CARVED AND INLAID MAHOGANY DISPLAY CABINET. With typical late Dublin inlaid details
and conventional bail handles. Victoria & Albert Museum. Crown Copyright.

PLATE 84

155   LATE CHIPPENDALE BURMA-PADAUK PIER CABINET.

PLATE 85

156 LATE CHIPPENDALE MAHOGANY BREAKFRONT SECRETARY CABINET.

PLATE 86

157   EARLY GEORGIAN GILT LEATHER AND PAINTED FOUR-FOLD SCREEN.

Index

[Italic figures refer to illustrations]